Countries of the World

Denmark

by Patricia J. Murphy

Consultant:
Marianne Stecher-Hansen
Associate Professor
Department of Scandinavian Studies
University of Washington

Bridgestone Books
an imprint of Capstone Press
Mankato, Minnesota

Bridgestone Books are published by Capstone Press
151 Good Counsel Drive, P.O. Box 669, Mankato, Minnesota 56002
http://www.capstone-press.com

Library of Congress Cataloging-in-Publication Data
Murphy, Patricia J., 1963–
    Denmark / by Patricia J. Murphy.
    p. cm.—(Countries of the world (Mankato, MN.))
    Includes bibliographical references and index.
    Summary: Introduces the geography, food, and culture of Denmark, including information
about the capital Copenhagen and author Hans Christian Andersen.
    ISBN 0-7368-1371-3 (hardcover)
    1. Denmark—Juvenile literature. [1. Denmark.] I. Title. II. Series.
DL109 .M87 2003
948.9—dc21   2001008368

Editorial Credits
Tom Adamson, editor; Karen Risch, product planning editor; Patrick D. Dentinger,
    book designer and illustrator; Alta Schaffer, photo researcher

Photo Credits
Betty Crowell, 8
Blaine Harrington III, 10
Bob Krist/CORBIS, 20
Danish Tourist Board, 14
Dave Bartruff/CORBIS, cover
Hulton-Deutsch Collection/CORBIS, 18
John La Due/Root Resources, 6
R. Fahnestock/HOME AT FIRST Travel, 16
StockHaus Limited, 5 (top)
TRIP/R. Powers, 12

Table of Contents

Name: Kingdom of Denmark

Capital: Copenhagen

Population: More than 5.3 million

Language: Danish

Religion: Evangelical Lutheran

Size: 16,639 square miles
(43,094 square kilometers)

Denmark is a little more than twice the size of the U.S. state of Massachusetts.

Crops: Grains, potatoes, sugar beets

Maps

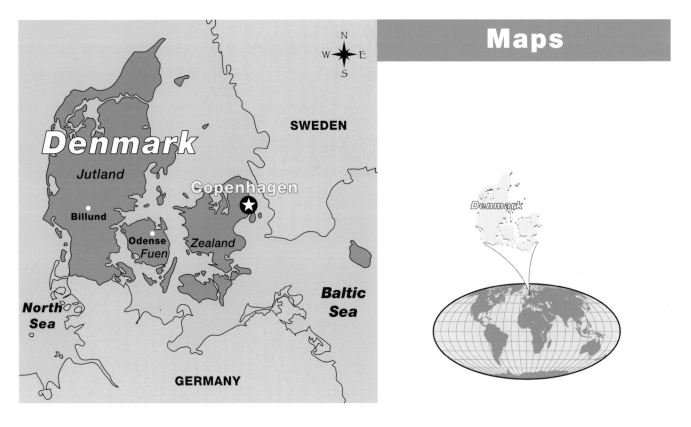

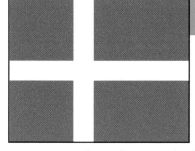

Flag

Denmark's flag is called Dannebrog. This name means "the spirit of Denmark." It is the world's oldest national flag. Denmark adopted the flag in the 1500s. The flag became the model for other Scandinavian country flags. These countries include Sweden, Norway, Finland, and Iceland. According to a legend, the Danish flag fell from the sky when Denmark's King Valdemar II defeated Estonia in 1219.

Currency

Denmark's unit of currency is the Danish krone. There are 100 øre in 1 krone.

In the early 2000s, about 8.5 kroner equaled 1 U.S. dollar. About 5.3 kroner equaled 1 Canadian dollar.

The Land

Denmark is a country in northern Europe. It is the smallest of the five Scandinavian countries.

Most of Denmark is on a peninsula called Jutland and on two main islands called Fuen and Zealand. It sits between the North and Baltic Seas. Denmark shares a border with Germany. Greenland and the Faeroe Islands also belong to Denmark.

Most of Denmark is flat. Rolling hills cover the center of the country. Sandy dunes and beaches lie along the coasts. Denmark also has more than 500 small islands.

Water surrounds Denmark, so its weather is mild and damp. Denmark's average rainfall is 28 inches (71 centimeters) each year. A lack of high hills or mountains makes Denmark very windy.

Winters are cold and snowy. Summers are sunny and warm. During June and July, the sun sets late at night, about 11:00. This happens because Denmark is so far north.

Rolling hills cover central Denmark.

Copenhagen

Copenhagen is Denmark's largest city. The city is located on the island of Zealand. Copenhagen became the capital of Denmark in 1443.

Denmark's Queen and her family live at Amalienborg Palace in Copenhagen. The Queen has no political power. She represents Denmark at public events. The Prime Minister heads the government. Denmark's government offices are also in Copenhagen.

Copenhagen's Tivoli Gardens opened in 1843. This amusement park is famous for its flowers and fountains. People can go on rides, attend concerts, and see displays of fireworks.

Near Copenhagen's harbor sits *The Little Mermaid* statue. The Little Mermaid is a character from a Hans Christian Andersen fairy tale. Andersen was a famous writer from Denmark. The statue honors his world-famous fairy tales.

The Little Mermaid statue is in Copenhagen.

Life at Home

Denmark has one of the highest standards of living in the world. Few Danes go without food, clothing, or housing.

The government helps the very young, old, sick, and people without jobs. It offers people free education, health care, and job training. This help is paid through taxes. More than half of Danes' income goes to pay taxes.

About 85 percent of Danes live in cities. They live in apartments or houses. They may tend cabbage patches outside the city. People plant vegetables, potatoes, and flowers in these small rented areas of land called kolonihaver. Many Danes also have vacation cottages in the country. The cabbage patches and vacation cottages allow Danes to escape the noisy, busy city.

The home is the center of Danish life. At home, Danes share hygge (HOO-gah) with family and friends. Hygge is a feeling of warmth and comfort.

Many Danes have cabbage patches outside the city.

Going to School

School is important to Danes. They believe education helps them live better lives. The government provides free schooling to all Danes.

At 6 years old, Danish children begin primary school, called Folkeskole. Students learn math, science, geography, and history. They also learn music, art, cooking, and physical education. Students study Danish, English, and German languages. They attend Folkeskole for nine or ten years.

After primary school, about half of Danish students choose a trade school. The other students choose secondary school or high school to prepare them for a university. These students must pass an exam to enter a university.

Many adults attend Folk High Schools. These schools help Danes continue learning. Adults attend Folk High Schools to learn more about culture, sports, history, art, or literature.

Danish children begin Folkeskole at age 6.

Danish Food

Danes often hurry through breakfast and lunch. But dinner is an important time. At this meal, Danes enjoy favorite foods with family and friends.

Breakfast may be coffee, tea, or rolls. Danes also eat Denmark's famous Wienerbrød. This pastry is made with butter, sliced almonds, and raisins. It is baked in a pretzel shape. Danes also might eat eggs, porridge, or cereal with milk.

Most Danes eat smørrebrød for lunch. These open-faced sandwiches are made with bread and butter. Danes top the buttered bread with fish, cold cuts, or cheese. They decorate the smørrebrød with sliced vegetables.

For dinner, Danes enjoy poultry, pork, fish, vegetables, salad, and potatoes. They also eat meatballs, called Frikadeller, with gravy and red beets. Many dinners include a warm dish and a "cold table." This table is filled with cold foods such as meats, vegetables, cheeses, and breads.

Smørrebrød are open-faced sandwiches.

Sports and Games

During winter, Danes enjoy ice skating outdoors. The country's small lakes and ponds freeze in winter. Indoors, Danes play card games and chess.

After long, cold winters, Danes head outdoors. The Danish countryside is perfect for bicycling. Its coastline gives Danes plenty of room to sail, swim, and row.

Soccer is Denmark's national sport. Children and adults watch and play soccer. Danes also play handball, tennis, and badminton.

Lego bricks were invented in Denmark in the 1930s by Ole Kirk Christiansen. These building toys were first made of wood. At Legoland in Billund, everything is made of Lego bricks. More than 1 million people visit Legoland every year.

Ice skating is a popular winter activity in Denmark.

Hans Christian Andersen

Hans Christian Andersen is Denmark's most famous writer. He wrote some of the world's most famous fairy tales. Three of these stories are "The Little Mermaid," "The Ugly Duckling," and "The Emperor's New Clothes."

Andersen was born in Odense in 1805. He was an only child. His father was a shoemaker. His mother was a washerwoman.

At age 14, Andersen left home for Copenhagen. He wanted to become an actor and singer. He had a nice voice, but he could not find work acting or singing.

To pay bills, he started writing. He sold stories to newspapers. He wrote a book about his childhood. In 1835, he wrote his first book of fairy tales. Some people liked them. His friends told him to keep writing fairy tales. These stories made Andersen famous. Today, people everywhere read his fairy tales.

Hans Christian Andersen wrote many famous fairy tales.

Holidays and Celebrations

Christmas is a favorite holiday in Denmark. They celebrate it for three days. The holiday begins on December 23 with Little Christmas Eve. On that day, Danish families decorate their homes and trees.

On Christmas Eve, Danes gather to eat their favorite foods and to open presents. They sing songs and dance around the Christmas tree. Danes dine on goose or pork and rice pudding. An almond is placed in the pudding. The person who finds it gets a prize. Finding the almond also means good luck for the coming year.

Danes celebrate New Year's Eve. They celebrate with fireworks and parties. They listen to speeches. They toast their friends by saying, "Skaal!" Some people play tricks on one another.

Danes celebrate Midsummer's Eve on June 23. This day has the most daylight of the year. They have bonfires and parties on beaches to celebrate the longest day.

Danes celebrate Midsummer's Eve with bonfires.

Hands On: Make Smørrebrød

Smørrebrød is a lunchtime favorite in Denmark. Try some of the Danes' favorite toppings or choose your own.

What You Need

Bread with hard crust (pumpernickel bread is preferred)
Knife
Butter
Butter knife
Hot or cold toppings
Plate

What You Do

1. Have an adult help you cut the bread into squares.
2. Spread butter on one side of the bread.
3. Top with your choice of parsley, pickles, onions, olives, tomatoes, onion rings, or whatever you like.
4. Serve on a plate.

Some of the favorite toppings used on smørrebrød in Denmark include roast beef, salami, eggs, ham, cheese, salmon, onions, shrimp, and eel. You may choose your own toppings for your smørrebrød. You could add bologna, turkey, or chicken.

Learn to Speak Danish

hello	goddag	(go-DAH)
good-bye	farvel	(FAH-vel)
yes	ja	(YA)
no	nej	(NEYE)
thank you	tak	(TAK)
you're welcome	selv tak	(SEL tak)
take it easy	bare rolig	(BAH-reh ROH-lig)

Words to Know

cottage (KOT-ij)—a small country house, usually used for vacations; Danes call them summer-houses.

legend (LEJ-uhnd)—a story handed down from earlier times

pastry (PAY-stree)—a light, flaky sweet roll

peninsula (puh-NIN-suh-luh)—an area of land surrounded by water on three sides

porridge (POR-ij)—a breakfast food made by boiling oats or other grains in milk or water until the mixture is thick

university (yoo-nuh-VUR-suh-tee)—a school that students go to after high school

Read More

Hansen, Ole Steen. *Denmark*. Country Insights. Austin, Texas: Raintree Steck-Vauhgn, 1998.

Hintz, Martin. *Denmark*. Enchantment of the World. Chicago: Children's Press, 1994.

Useful Addresses and Internet Sites

Danish Tourist Board
655 Third Avenue, 18th Floor
New York, NY 10017

Royal Danish Embassy
3200 Whitehaven Street NW
Washington, DC 20008-3683

CIA—The World Factbook—Denmark
http://www.odci.gov/cia/publications/factbook/geos/da.html
Legoland
http://www.lego.com/legoland/billund/defaultus.asp

Index